MW01155180

Baby Cake

An Egg Donation Story

Once upon a time, in a land far away, there lived a nice woman named Jordan and her kind husband, Josh.

They had a wonderful life together.

They had family who loved them.

They had cute and furry pets.

They had a cozy home.

But there was one thing that felt missing from their lives…..a baby of their own, for them to love.

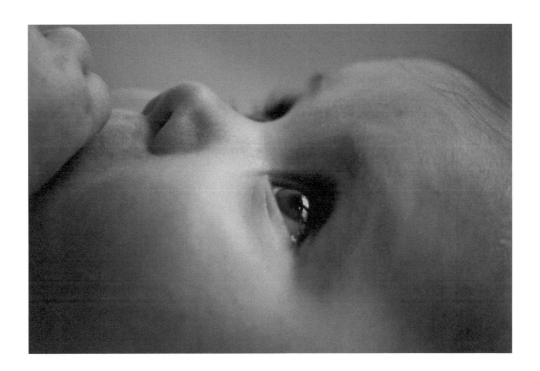

So, they decided to ask God to help them make a baby. And God answered them! God told them that to make a baby; you need an egg, flour, lots of love, and an oven. Jordan and Josh were so excited! They already had the flour, the oven, and all the love in the world for their baby, but they didn't have an egg!

"Oh, no!" said Jordan, "We need an egg to help us make our baby, but I don't have any. And only ladies have eggs. How will we make our baby if we don't have the egg?" Josh had an idea. "Don't worry, he said. "We'll ask a nice lady if she has an extra egg that we can have, to make our baby!" Jordan smiled. "Good idea!" and they gave each other a high five and a big hug!

So Jordan and Josh asked lots of nice ladies if any of them had an egg that they could have, to help them make their baby. Because people are so kind and giving, they all wanted to help them, and give them an egg! They were so helpful, sweet and kind. Jordan and Josh couldn't pick ALL of the eggs, so they decided together on a very nice, beautiful and kind lady, who was overjoyed to give them an egg, to help them make their very own Baby Cake!

The next day, Jordan and Josh took their flour, oven, egg and all of their love, and mixed it all together to make their baby cake. They put the baby cake in Jordan's tummy, and the egg, flour, oven, and love turned the baby cake into Jordan and Josh's BABY!

And their baby grew STRONG!

And their baby grew BIG!

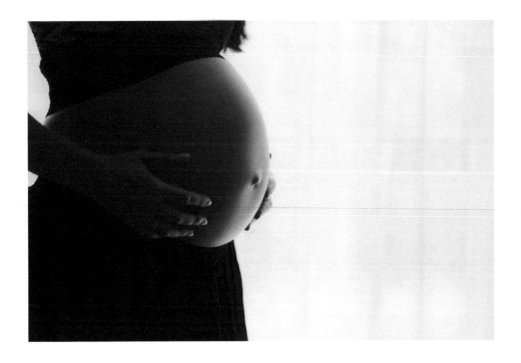

And the bigger their baby got, the bigger Mommy's tummy got!

And their baby loved hearing Jordan, their mommy, sing to them!

And their baby loved hearing Josh, their daddy, talk to them!

And one day, when their baby was ready, out they came from their mommy's belly! What a happy day!

And their mommy and daddy fed their baby, changed their diapers, sang to them, and loved to hear their little laugh. They are a family!

And guess who their baby in this story is? It's YOU!

You are our wonderful and loved baby. And we wanted you SO much!

Now that we have you, we love playing with you!

We love teaching you things!

We love giving you hugs!

We love taking care of you!

And we love our family!

And to think, it's all because Mommy and Daddy decided to bake a Baby Cake! We are so grateful that you made us a family. We love being your mommy and daddy. We love you very much. We are so glad that God blessed us with you!

Love, Your Mommy and Daddy

CPSIA information can be obtained
at www.ICGtesting.com
Printed in the USA
LVHW072131251118
598231LV00018B/596/P